CW00695930

DRINK LIKE THE SWISS

BY: ANDIE PILOT

♥ For Sam ♥
the world's best
drinking buddy

ISBN 978-3-03869-049-8

FSC
www.fsc.org
MIX
Papier aus ver-
antwortungsvollen
Quellen
FSC® C083411

DRINK à la SWISS

The famous French Renaissance philosopher and essayist Michel de Montaigne wrote in his essay "On Experience" (*De l'Expérience*):

> You make a German ill if you force him to lie on a mattress, as you do an Italian on a feather bed, or a Frenchman without bed curtains or a fire. A Spaniard's stomach cannot tolerate the way we eat, nor ours the way the Swiss drink.

The Swiss were notorious heavy drinkers during Montaigne's time and although their reputation has faded, a rich drinking tradition continues throughout the country. Those who think of the Swiss as mild-mannered and temperate, have never been to a Basler Fasnacht, a Fête de Vendages, or the meeting of pretty much any Swiss student fraternity.

One of the world's most infamous spirits, absinthe, originated in French speaking Switzerland's Val-de-Travers. Swiss farmers make spirits with every possible fruit on their farms, as well as potatoes and hay. In the mountains, alpine herbs and even the beloved edelweiss flavour the *Schnaps*.

But it's not just about booze. The Swiss are not only brewers, vintners, and distillers, they are also some of the world's leading coffee exporters, dairy farmers, and ice tea fanatics. Mark Twain, during his travels through the country, filled his canteen with fresh Swiss milk and drank the "exquisitely cold water" spilling from the glaciers.

They've perfected hot chocolate, put milk in their soda, made the world's best beer, and harvested the world's smallest vineyard.

So raise a glass, and let's drink like the Swiss.

TABLE of CONTENTS

TABLE of CONTENTS

You too can drink like the Swiss!

The intention of this book is to provide an overview of Swiss drinks and drinking habits. You'll find traditional recipes from grandmothers and farmers, classic cocktails given a Swiss twist, and new drinks using the best ingredients that Switzerland has to offer.

The recipes in this book, whether for everyday or for celebrations, have been loosely organised into the times of day that they are enjoyed: dawn, midday, and dusk (though this is only a suggestion and no one, certainly not the Swiss, will discourage you from adding *Schnaps* to your morning brew).

But it's not just about what the Swiss drink, but how they drink it. Whether it's caramel *Schnaps* as a reward for the back-breaking labour of making linen by hand, a sweet cherry love potion made by farmers' daughters and served to bachelors on New Year's Eve, or heavily spiced wine pouring out of a fountain in Basel to ring in the new year, the Swiss tie drink to all aspects of daily life and celebration.

BOOZY TERMINOLOGY

The word *Schnaps* in German refers to any strong, distilled spirit. Although *Schnaps* can be flavoured, it typically has a higher alcohol content (around 40%).

The cherry or peach "schnapps" often sold in the English speaking realm are actually liqueurs, heavily sweetened and flavoured, with a lower percentage of alcohol (around 15-30%).

For tips on Schnaps *making and cocktail shaking, see page 92.*

MILKandCOFFEE

Plenty of Swiss drink two of the country's most important commercial products every morning—milk and coffee.

Dairy farming makes up a fifth of Switzerland's agriculture, and the Swiss consume on average just over 70 litres of milk per person, per year, which places them in the top five of milk consuming nations, per capita.

Alpine agriculture became prominent throughout the Swiss Alps in the Middle Ages. Over time, gentle cows, grazing in flower-filled alpine pastures and producing wholesome and delicious milk, would become one of the iconic representations of the country.

The country has excellent infrastructure to bring milk—their white gold— to the masses. There are pipelines transporting it directly from cows in alpine pastures to processing plants below, and in some communities there are even vending machines providing it, fresh and creamy, at any hour of the day.

Another important export is coffee and Switzerland is currently the fifth largest coffee exporter in the world. The Swiss themselves love their brew—they consistently rank in the top ten of coffee drinking nations.

That's some way to start the day.

AUTOMATIC COFFEE

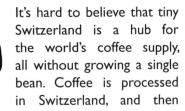

It's hard to believe that tiny Switzerland is a hub for the world's coffee supply, all without growing a single bean. Coffee is processed in Switzerland, and then exported to other nations. Incredibly, the Swiss export more coffee than they do chocolate or cheese.

NESCAFÉ

It's been to the moon and back, as well as to the earth's highest summit. The world's first soluble powdered coffee was introduced in Switzerland by Nestlé in 1938. It was a way to preserve Brazil's overabundant coffee bean harvests and it met with immediate success. Though it would probably not be the drink of choice for real coffee lovers, Nescafé is sold in nearly every country in the world, and it remains popular to this day.

NESPRESSO

By 1976, Nestlé engineer Eric Favre had already invented the Nespresso capsule system. Although it took almost three decades, Nespresso now dominates home coffee capsule brewing. There are boutiques in nearly 70 countries throughout the world, though all the coffee in Nespresso capsules is roasted and ground exclusively in Switzerland.

MILCHKAFFE

My grandmother, like many Swiss, made *Milchkaffee* (strong, milky coffee) for every breakfast and dinner. She'd fill two ceramic jugs, one with steamed milk and the other with her special coffee blend (a mixture of coffee and chicory, sometimes sweetened, sometimes not), which would be drunk from little bowls called *Chacheli*. Due to the strength of the coffee, about half of the cup would be filled with milk.

CHICORY

As coffee was traditionally an expensive product, most people could not afford to drink it pure. Many kinds of cheaper plants and grains were roasted and added to coffee—or during very lean times they replaced coffee entirely.

One of these plants was chicory, which has been produced as a coffee substitute in Switzerland since at least the early 1800s. After the Second World War, it became easier to get coffee, but many producers still added chicory for its subtle flavour and rich black colour. Many Swiss, including my grandmother and mother-in-law, recognise it as an integral part of their morning brew.

To make your own *Milchkaffee*, use a mix of ground coffee and chicory—or you can buy pre-mixed chicory coffee in most Swiss supermarkets. My mother-in-law, Josy, gave me these tips: keep the water just under the boiling point to prevent the coffee from getting bitter, the milk should also not boil, and once you're done with the coffee grounds, add them to your garden—they make excellent fertilizer.

Josy's MILCHKAFFEE

Stovetop

Heat 2 litres water and coffee to just under boiling.

Take off the heat and leave the grounds to settle, then ladle or pour the coffee into a jug.

150-200g ground coffee
1 tbsp chicory

Coffee filter

Add coffee to filter

Heat 2 litres water in a kettle and just before it boils, gradually pour it through the filter.

Warm, but don't boil a litre of milk.

add to a jug.

serve immediately.

a skin tends to form on the hot milk, so use a sieve when pouring.

Typical ratio of coffee to milk is one to one.

OVOMALTINE

In the middle of the 1800s, every fifth child in Switzerland died of malnutrition. Wanting to combat the problem, the pharmacist and chemist Georg Wander, and later his son Albert, experimented with malt in their Bernese laboratory. Eventually they succeeded in making Ovomaltine, a mix-in-milk powder made from malt, egg, and milk, and flavoured with cocoa.

During the Second World War, drinking Ovomaltine was seen as an act of national solidarity, as well as an important source of nutrition for children. Today, the Swiss supply is still produced in the original factory in Neuenegg, near Bern, and the original recipe remains largely unchanged.

Swiss advertisements throughout the decades have consistently shown Ovomaltine, combined with alpine milk and outdoor activities, to be the key to good health. Their famous tongue-in-cheek slogan *Mit Ovo chaschs nöd besser. Aber länger!* ("With Ovo you can't do it better, but you can do it longer!") spawned dozens of print and TV ads.

With factories all over the world, Ovo is appreciated by an international clientele. Today it is estimated that three billion cups are drunk every year worldwide.

(And no, English speakers, that's not a spelling mistake—the original name of the product was misspelled on its British trademark registration, leading to its English name of Ovaltine.)

To temper the healthiness,
  why not add a scoop of ice cream?

OVOMALTINE *milkshake*

200 ml milk
1 tbsp ovomaltine powder
1 scoop vanilla ice cream

blend until smooth and
top with whipped cream

MALT on MALT *float*

mix 200 ml stout
with 1 tbsp
ovomaltine powder

top with a big scoop
of vanilla ice cream

a good
choice for
stout is
Schwarzer
Kristall
from
Appenzeller
Bier

DRINKING CHOCOLATE

The Swiss didn't invent the chocolate drink—the Mayans were already drinking their bitter brew centuries ago. But nowadays, who would you expect to make better drinkable chocolate than the Swiss? The addition of milk from happy, well-fed cows only serves to make creamy chocolate more luxurious.

A good hot chocolate can be rich and thick, almost tempting you to eat it with a spoon, or it can be slightly lighter, allowing you to drink it fast and warm up quickly. The best chocolate drinks demand using the best (Swiss) chocolate or cocoa powder that you can find.

COCOA

whisk together:

pinch of salt.

dribble of vanilla (paste or extract)

200 ml milk

1 tbsp cocoa powder

2 tsp sugar

Warm over medium heat, but don't boil.

decadent
HOT CHOCOLATE

Measure out:
30ml cream
200ml milk

Chop:
30g dark chocolate
20g milk chocolate

Heat a third of the milk mixture until bubbling.

Whisk in the chocolate and a pinch of salt, then the rest of the milk.

quick
HOT CHOCOLATE

Place three Lindor balls in a mug.

whisk in 200ml hot milk.

MILK

Taking the cows up to the Alps in the summer and letting them graze on fresh alpine meadows has a positive influence on the flavour of Swiss milk. But that's not the only reason the milk tastes so good.

Switzerland has some of the strictest animal welfare regulations in the world, and the farms are regularly inspected. On average, each farm has only around 23 cows, making it easier to take care of those animals and to spread them over the available land.

Take Fiona here (that's probably her name, it's the top name for cows in Switzerland). Each day she'll eat about 100 kg of meadow grasses, 2 kg of feed, 200 g salt, and drink 50 litres of water and produce about 20-25 litres of milk.

And when Fiona has calves of her own, according to my veterinarian father-in-law Robi, she will be rewarded with one of the Swiss farmer's treasured drinks: *Kafischnaps* (just what it sounds like: coffee with *Schnaps*). In French-speaking Switzerland, the new bovine mums also get a taste of the farmer's preferred tipple—a bottle of good wine. As Robi said, they've earned it.

HONIGMILCH

Whisk a tsp wildflower honey into 200ml hot milk.

Mix your milk with some wildflower honey for a taste of alpine meadows.

FROM WATER to WINE

All manner of drinks grace Swiss tables throughout the day—water, soft drinks, ice tea, beer, wine.

Water is the basis for all other drinks, though the Swiss also like theirs plain (and still, which is more popular than sparkling), consuming over 100 litres per person, per year.

Switzerland is awash with mineral-rich wells sometimes springing from deep in the mountains. Initially it was apothecaries and doctors who used this kind of water therapeutically. They also experimented by adding different curatives and flavourings, resulting in the creation of many soft drinks.

The temperance movement in the early 20th century helped promote the consumption of non-alcoholic beverages over liquor, and from the 1950s onwards, mineral water and soft drinks, as well as juice, were seen as healthy alternatives to alcoholic drinks.

However, the Swiss are great consumers of beer and wine as well.

There are currently around a thousand registered beer breweries in the country, giving Switzerland the highest (registered) brewer to citizen ratio in the world. And as for wine, although the Swiss export hardly any bottles, they continue to maintain their top ten finish in wine consumption per capita.

CHÖRBLIWASSER

The slightly sparkling *Chörbliwasser* is a twice-distilled drink that tastes of liquorice and is used medicinally. The flavour comes from the addition of *myrrhis odorata*, or sweet cicely, and it was traditionally prepared in two disparate regions of Switzerland—the Rhein valley in St. Gallen, and the Emmental in Bern.

Chörbliwasser has been applied to rashes and other skin conditions, as well as to open wounds as a mild disinfectant. Dentists would suggest their patients gargle it to relieve infections in the mouth. And some enthusiasts still drink it daily, claiming it purifies their blood and lowers blood pressure.

SIRUP

Go to any Swiss cafe with a small child and they will probably be offered a glass of *Sirup*. The flavours vary, but *Sirup* remains a firm favourite with children and adults alike.

Holunderblütensirup / sirop de fleurs de sureau / sciroppo di fiori di sambuco (elderflower syrup) is a syrup of many uses. In Switzerland, it is added with abandon to sparking water, wine, or cocktails like Hugo, for a light and floral summery taste.

ELDERFLOWER Syrup

Collect 5 stems of elderflower — look for freshly opened buds.

Shake off bugs *

Swirl gently in cold water.

200 ml water
200 g sugar
bring to a boil

Take off the heat and add half a lemon, sliced, and the elderflower.

— flowers first, stems sticking up

cover the pot and let sit for a day or so.

Strain and keep in the fridge for up to 3 weeks. Makes 300 ml.

HUGO

Though it didn't originate here, Hugo is one of Switzerland's favourite summer drinks.

It happened just across the border—Roland Gruber, a beardy, south Tirolean vagabond barkeep, mixed together *Zitronenmelissensirup* (lemon balm syrup), Prosecco, mint, and a spritz of soda water, thought up a name off the top of his head, and served it to regulars at his bar in Naturns in 2005.

Other than a bit of notoriety, Gruber didn't really get any compensation for creating what would become one of the most ubiquitous drinks in the German-speaking realm. By 2010, it had spread from Sylt to Schwyz and was a standard summer cocktail at bars, restaurants, and hotels.

The ingredients have changed slightly, with many bartenders preferring *Holunderblütensirup* (elderflower syrup), adding lime, and some replacing the Prosecco with white wine or champagne.

Today it remains a refreshing classic on a warm summer's day.

HUGO

3 mint leaves

1 tbsp elderflower syrup

ice

150 mL sparkling wine

sparkling water

lime

Muddle the mint in a wine glass, then add ice. Add elderflower syrup and sparkling wine. Top with sparkling water. Stir. Garnish with lime and more mint.

prosseco.

RIVELLA

Of course the national soda pop of Switzerland is made with milk.

First produced in 1952, Rivella is one of Switzerland's most iconic drinks. Its name is a mix of the Italian word *rivelazione* (revelation) and the Ticino town of Riva San Vitale. It's made from milk serum (also known as whey), herb and fruit tea extract, water, sugar and fizz.

The whey is what makes the drink particularly Swiss. For centuries, dairy farmers enjoyed drinking this by-product of cheese production. This was later adopted as a health product by early Swiss nutritionists. In the 1800s, health tourists to Swiss sanitariums were taking whey baths.

The whey that's used in today's Rivella is more processed than the unfiltered product of the past. However, much like another famous Swiss drink, Ovomaltine, its connection with overall health, outdoor living, and its so-called nutritional advantages are still heavily advertised—and highly dubious.

On average, the Swiss drink around 10 litres of Rivella per person, per year.

RIVELLUM

2 parts rum
1 part lemon juice
4 parts Rivella
stir over ice.

RIVA SAN VITALE

Some Italian favourites appear
in this Ticino inspired cocktail

1 part nocino
1 part grappa
5 parts Rivella
stir over ice.

SWISS SOFT DRINKS

GAZOSA

These colourful flavoured sparkling waters from Ticino have been around since the end of the 19th century. Called "poor man's champagne" because the bottles made a similar pop when opened, *gazosa* initially relied on natural fermentation to create its bubbles. Today the flavours—everything from indigo alpine blueberry to bitter orange—are simply added to carbonated water.

PEPITA

Switzerland's grapefruit soda has been around since 1929. The water used to make the drink comes from Eptigen, near Basel, a famous spring renowned for its medicinal properties.

ELMER CITRO

Elmer Citro is Switzerland's best-known lemon pop. Its recipe has not changed since 1927, when production began at the Elm spring in canton Glarus. The water from this spring has been bottled and bathed in since the Middle Ages, and it remains the exclusive source of water for the Elmer Citro drink.

SCHWEPPES

And none of these drinks could have existed without the ingenuity of another Swiss inventor, Johann Jacob Schweppe, who used the research of Joseph Priestley to develop a practical process to add the bubbles to fizzy drinks. From there, his company Schweppes came to life.

le PAMPLEMOUSSE

1 part elderflower syrup

3 parts gin

10 parts Pepita

Stir over ice.

The classic North American children's drink Shirley Temple was named for the actress who brought the prototypical Swiss Miss, Heidi, to the masses.

HEIDI

1 tbsp grenadine or raspberry syrup

Top with Elmer Citro

Garnish with a maraschino cherry

Heidi's grandfather always struck me as a man who would enjoy a tipple now and then.

HEIDI'S GRANDFATHER

Make a Heidi, spike with Kirsch.

ICE TEA

Check your local *Badi*, or swimming hole, and you're bound to find bottles littered next to nearly every towel. Of ice tea, that is.

Ice tea, and particularly the variety sold from Migros, has been a cult Swiss product for over thirty years, but before the early eighties, ice tea wasn't available commercially. It was after a trip to the States that one of the founders, Ruedi Bärlocher, decided to brew a batch and test it with the Swiss populous. With partner Max Sprenger, they made 2000 litres, filled tetra packs, and hit the shelves.

The Swiss loved it.

Today, they remain the largest consumer of ice tea in Europe, guzzling around 30 litres per person, per year (compare that to the next highest, the Belgians, who consume only about 10 litres). Migros alone produces nearly 70 million litres a year, in a variety of flavours—from alpine herbs to rhubarb—though classic blue remains the favourite.

ALPINE ICE TEA

So maybe you can't get your hands on fresh edelweiss, but there are plenty of alpine herbs that you can use to make a floral and refreshing alpine tea. And fortunately, you can buy alpine herb tea bags in any supermarket in the country.

For a taste of the Alps, follow the recipe for the ice tea syrup on the following page. You can use this as a base for ice tea (just dilute with water to your desired sweetness), or use it in mixed drinks and punches in place of sugar syrup.

ALPINE TEA

Alpine teas often contain these plants:

chamomile

sage

rose hip

thyme

gentian root

peppermint

lemon balm

verbena

lady's mantle

nettles

edelweiss

ALPINE ICE TEA SYRUP

Boil 400ml water and the juice and peel of 2 lemons.

Reduce heat and add:

4 alpine herb tea bags
2 black tea bags

Simmer 10 minutes then remove tea bags and lemon peel.

Add 300g sugar and simmer until it dissolves.

Strain into a bottle.

Let cool, then store in the fridge for up to 3 weeks.

Makes about 500mL.

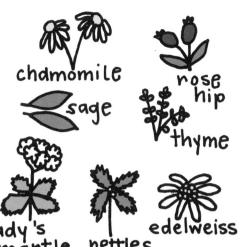

Alpine ice tea syrup

MOST

Freshly pressed apple (and pear) juice can be found all over Switzerland in the fall, from your local market to your local Migros. Although the fresh juice is particularly delicious, today much of the product is pasteurized, bottled, and available year-round.

Referred to as *Most* or *Moscht* in German speaking Switzerland (*cidre* in French), the apple juice can be non-alcoholic, as in *Süssmost*, or alcoholic, as in *saurer Most* (though to make it very confusing, alcohol-free *suure Most* is also available). The name *Most* is from the Latin word for freshly pressed grapes, *vinum mustum.*

Saurer Most stems from at least the Middle Ages, when farmers would make vinegar and lightly alcoholic drinks with their apple juice. Apple juice naturally ferments after a few days, so it wasn't until the early 1900s when pasteurization made it possible for the non-alcoholic version to be stored and sold at market.

Süssmost then became popular with children and athletes—and the government, who were trying to combat alcoholism. Even during poor harvests, much of the fruit was being used to make alcoholic drinks, so the government tried to encourage the production and consumption of the softer variety of juice.

A variation on the theme is the *Schorle*—which just indicates that the juice is diluted with a bit of water, most often sparkling and sometimes still. *Schorles* exist in as many variations as there are fruits, with apple being the most popular.

GLÜHMOST

This is a wonderful alternative for children who can't drink the heady and alcoholic *Glühwein* of the Christmas season (though you can always use boozy cider if the occasion demands).

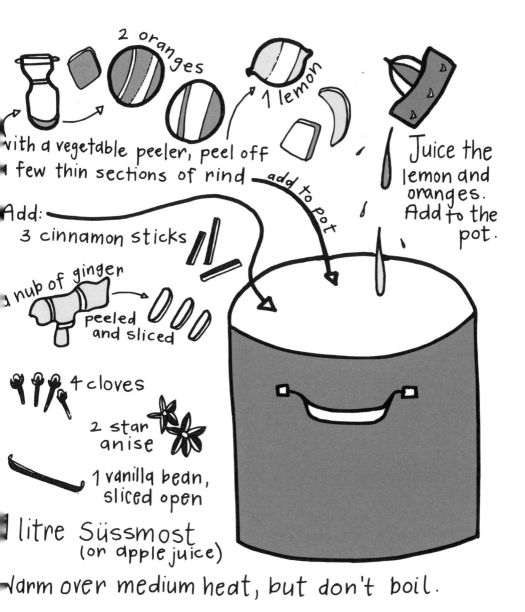

2 oranges

1 lemon

with a vegetable peeler, peel off a few thin sections of rind — add to pot

Juice the lemon and oranges. Add to the pot.

Add:

3 cinnamon sticks

a nub of ginger, peeled and sliced

4 cloves

2 star anise

1 vanilla bean, sliced open

1 litre Süssmost (or apple juice)

Warm over medium heat, but don't boil.

MONASTERY MICROBREW

It was monastery dwellers who developed a rich brewing tradition in medieval Europe, including those at the Abbey of St Gallen.

Today, its library is a treasure trove of medieval rarities. This includes the ninth century Plan of St. Gall, the best-preserved architectural plan of a Middle Age abbey— which included three large, elaborate brew houses. Although it was never actually built, it's interpreted as an example of an ideal monastic complex, and one where beer brewing played a central role in the nourishment of the monks.

the SWISS BEER CARTEL

Flash forward a thousand years—in 1890 there were about 500 domestic breweries in Switzerland. But by 1998 this had dwindled to 24. So what happened?

An association of brewers, the *Schweizerischer Bierbrauerverein*, was founded in 1887. After the financial collapse following the First World War, the association lobbied successfully to impose high taxes on imported beers. By 1935, they had enough control of the market to write their own convention. The organization worked as a cartel controlling everything from beer distribution, to the size of bottles and ingredients used. Restaurants, hotels, shops, and supermarkets were forced into exclusive contracts.

What was initially seen as a protection of Swiss beer, eventually became its undoing. With no reason to change and no competition, innovation suffered, and so did the beer. Finally, in the 1990s, the cartel collapsed and foreign beers flooded the market, providing consumers with a better choice. Ironically, almost all of the cartel breweries were bought by foreign companies like Heineken and Carlsberg, the very thing they had tried to avoid less than a century before.

BEER on TAP
vom FASS
à la PRESSION
alla SPINA

For a standard lager beer in German-speaking Switzerland, ordering a **Stange** will get you around 300ml.

Other names you might see on a menu:

200 ml

Herrgöttli
Galopin
Flûte

300 ml

Chübeli
Rugeli

500 ml

Grosses
Chöbu/Kübel

Mass
Litron
Krug

1 Litre

SWISS CRAFT BEER

At their weakest, the breweries may have numbered 24, but the rebuilding of the Swiss beer market, in tandem with a worldwide surge in craft beer sales, has meant a growth of microbreweries. According to the Swiss register of brewers, there are around a thousand active breweries registered in Switzerland today.

Although the big breweries of the past still seem to dominate, Swiss craft beer is a small but thriving scene. Located in seemingly every *Scheune* and *Spycher* (barn and storehouse) in the country, there is a local brewery near you that is worth exploring.

BFM

There are far too many great brewers to mention, though the one exception is *Brasserie de Franches Montagnes*, or BFM, the grandfather of craft beer in Switzerland. Its founder, Jérôme Rebetez finished a degree in Viticulture with the goal of making a brewery in his home region, the Jura. He succeeded, and the brewery opened in 1997. Brewed using traditional cask methods, as well as occasional unconventional ingredients (lapsang souchong tea, sarawak peppers), the beers of BFM have received international acclaim. In 2009, their *L'Abbaye de Saint Bon-Chien* was declared the best beer in the world by *The New York Times*.

Although it probably won't win you any friends in craft beer circles, there's something to be said for a refreshing

PANACHÉ

Mix equal parts light beer (weizen, pilsner, lager) with lemon soda (sprite, 7up).

Pilsner
=
light
and
earthy

weizen
=
smooth
and
rich

Lager
=
fresh
and
light

WINE in SWITZERLAND

If you live outside Switzerland you might not know that the Swiss make some truly excellent wine. That's because nearly all of their wine is consumed within Switzerland—less than 3% makes it out of the country.

Switzerland has some indigenous grapes, and some that may have origins elsewhere but are grown pretty much exclusively here. These unique varieties are worth seeking out:

WHITE

Introduced by the Romans **AMIGNE** is citrusy and fresh with a nice sweetness
valais

Thought to be high in iron and once given to mothers who had just given birth **HUMAGNE BLANC** is citrusy & light
valais

The ambassador of Valais wine **PETITE ARVINE** is fruity with light bitterness
valais

The pearl of alpine wine **HEIDA/PAÏEN** is full-bodied but fresh
valais

RED

Recently ressurected **CORNALIN** is fruity and mellows with age
valais

The wild and rustic offspring of cornalin is **HUMAGNE ROUGE** full-bodied & full of character
valais

Two very rare grapes that are making a comeback are **HIMBERTSCHA** and **LAFNETSCHA** wild & unpredictable
valais

The rare **COMPLETER** dates from 1321 and is rich, strong and full of character
graybunden

how to KEEP your WINE STRAIGHT

Here are some of the most popular swiss wines and their aliases. (confusingly there are often more than one name for the same wine)
If it's a regional name, the canton is given.

In Switzerland, these two grapes are often made into sweet wines:

Marsanne / Ermitage (VS)

Pinot Gris / Malvoisie (VS)

For all your melted cheese needs:
Chasselas / Fendant / Gutedel / Perlan / Dorin
(VS) (GE) (VD)

The light and musky, swiss invented crossbreed:
Müller-Thurgau / Riesling × Sylvaner

Spargelzeit (asparagus season) demands:
Sylvaner / Johannisberg (VS)

The classic from Ticino:
Merlot

(try the white variety Merlot Bianco if you get a chance)

The smooth blend of Pinot Noir and Gamay:
Dôle

Peppery and fruity:
Pinot Noir / Blauburgunder / Clevner
(ZH)

MUNICIPAL WINE COLLECTIONS

During my husband's time at the University of Bern, he was occasionally called upon to help with the organisation of an event. Sponsorship would be requested from different associations and he could be pretty sure that there would be an offering from the city of Bern—in the form of wine.

Bern isn't the only municipality with its own vineyard, and depending where you are, the quality of the wines can be phenomenal—take for example Aigle, a famous wine producing town in Vaud where they happily sell their *Vin de Commune* to the public.

the highest VINEYARD in EUROPE

The idea of a collective wine supply is hardly recent, as small plots of vineyards have been pooling their resources for centuries.

Take the Valaisian families who own the highest vineyard in Europe at Visperterminen. Different owners maintain various parts (and sizes) of these historic vines, which sit as high as 1150m above sea level, and they typically pick the grapes themselves, by hand, as the height and slope prevent mechanised harvesting.

The grapes are processed and sold by the cooperative St. Jodern Kellerei, an association set up and overseen by the families. The pearl of the wines they produce is Heida, which thrives under the sun in high altitudes.

VIN des GLACIERS
the oldest Swiss wine

High in the mountains of Valais you will find the *Vin des Glaciers*, wine in barrels that are never fully emptied.

Since at least the 18th century, alpine nomads have been filling their larch barrels with each year's wine, then cellaring it in mountain villages. Also called the sherry of the Alps, today some drops of this golden liquid are over 125 years old.

The wine isn't sold, rather it's drunk by the vintners on occasions that warrant it—births, weddings, funerals. Occasionally, a lucky outside few are able to taste the wine—in the small town of Grimetz in the Val d'Anniviers.

SAUSER/VIN BOURRU
the youngest Swiss wine

I've made the common mistake with *Sauser*. Despite my husband reminding me not to tip the bottle, it found its way onto its side and splash, all our groceries were covered in grape juice.

Sauser is a fermented, slightly sparkling, freshly-pressed grape juice that is available to buy during the grape harvest. Initially it contains about 4% alcohol, which increases the longer it sits in your fridge, topping out at about 10%.

Because this young wine has begun its fermentation process, gasses are constantly escaping from the bottle. To allow these to escape without the bottle exploding, the lids are loose, with air holes.

Sauser doesn't keep well, so it's best to drink it (cool, out of the fridge) quickly.

OEIL de PERDRIX

Oeil de Perdrix (French for "eye of the partridge") is a rosé wine made from Pinot Noir grapes that is a speciality of Neuchâtel.

It was this wine that led to the most profound and polemic wine revolution in the United States—the rise of White Zinfandel. White Zinfandel is a sweet pink wine that oenophiles love to hate. However, in the late 1980s it became the best-selling wine in America, and its creator was praised for introducing wine to more Americans than ever before.

So what does White Zin have to do with Oeil de Perdrix?

Sutter Home Winery in Northern California was founded by Swiss immigrants, then purchased by Italian brothers after the Second World War. The brothers tried their hand at making an Oeil de Perdrix style wine, using California's favourite red grape, Zinfandel.

A couple of years into their experimentation, one of their batches failed due to stuck fermentation (when the yeast dies before it has converted all of the sugars into alcohol), so the wine was put aside. Two weeks later they were pleased to discover that the sweet pink drink tasted delicious.

Although they attempted to call it Oeil de Perdrix, the Bureau of Alcohol, Tobacco and Firearms thought the name would be too confusing to the American public, so the vintners just named it after the grape, calling the pink wine White Zinfandel.

Ironically, although the wine snobs thought the White Zin was an over-sweet, pedestrian wine, it was because of its popularity that many old Zinfandel vines were preserved and would later be used to create impressive red Zinfandels in the 1990s.

OEIL de PERDRIX
Bellini

add stone fruit purée to a glass

top with chilled Oeil de Perdrix stir

MAKE YOUR OWN
stone fruit purée

add pitted, cut fruit to a pot

boil down until you have a thick sauce

buzz with an immersion blender

strain, if desired

garnish with lime

HYPOKRAS

It's in Basel where Hypokras, festive spiced wine, is most beloved today—so much so that it pours from their *Dreizackbrunnen*, a famous fountain, on New Year's Day. With a glass in one hand and a *Basler Läckerli* in the other, it's the perfect way to start the year off right.

Place the following into a large pot:

2 cinnamon sticks

50g sugar

3 slices of ginger

3 cloves

2 lemons, sliced

1 cup black tea

3 oranges, sliced

a bottle of white wine

a bottle of red wine

Warm over medium heat, but don't boil.

Hypokras is the spicier, fruitier version, of mulled wine. The recipes on the following page focus more on the wine itself, so pick ones that you actually like to drink.

GLÜHWEIN

3 peppercorns

2 cloves

2 cardamom pods

a grating of nutmeg

a tsp. vanilla paste

2 slices of ginger

2 cinnamon sticks

a bottle of red wine

2 tbsp brown sugar

a bay leaf

Warm over medium heat, but don't boil.

VIN BLANC CHAUD

2 oranges and 2 lemons, sliced

2 cinnamon sticks

3 star anise

30 g honey

a bottle of white wine

warm over medium heat, but don't boil.

the WORLD's
smallest VINEYARD

High in the Valaisian Alps, the smallest vineyard in the world is made up of three vines and named for a famous counterfeiter. *La vigne à Farinet* (Farinet's vineyard) is only 1.618 m2, slightly larger than a queen-sized bed. Its name serves as tribute to the man who has been dubbed the "Robin Hood of the Alps".

Born in Aosta in 1845, Joseph-Samuel Farinet was a lively drinker and womanizer who made his fortune counterfeiting money. On the run from Italian authorities, he hid among the peasants of the Valais and continued his crime, forging 20 *Rappen* pieces. But he was also a generous rogue who shared his counterfeited money with the locals, lifting them out of debt and improving their lives. They mourned in 1880 when his body was found in a gorge near Saillon, and today he remains a symbol of the wild heart of the region.

It was Jean-Louis Barrault, a French actor who portrayed Farinet in a film from the 1930s, who founded the Friends of Farinet and conceived of the tiny vineyard as a place for people to retreat from the stresses of modern life. He would eventually give the vineyard to Abbé Pierre, a Catholic priest famed for fighting in the French Resistance and founding Emmaus, who in turn gave the property to the Dalai Lama in 1999.

Each year, notable people work the land—everyone from Jane Birkin and Claudia Cardinale, to Michael Schumacher and Roger Moore. All the bottles produced (1000 per year, supplemented with grapes from nearby vineyards) are sold to raise money for charity.

WHEN the SPIRITS COME OUT

Alchemy—its goals were straightforward: find a universal solvent, find the elixir of life, turn lead into gold.

Alchemists were determined to extract the "spirit" of a liquid in a bid to find its essence, and possibly the elixir of life. After learning about distillation from Arab scholars, Europeans began the process of separating the alcohol from fermented beverages—first turning wine into brandy.

The name for this distillate came from the Latin for water of life, *aqua vitae*, like the Italian *aqua vite* or French *eau-de-vie*. In German, it can be called *Geist*, spirit, or *Branntwein*, literally burned wine, referring to the distillation process.

In the Middle Ages, spirits were the domain of doctors and apothecaries, and used primarily for medicinal purposes. But as time passed, spirits made their way into restaurants, into bars, and into the home.

But spirits were not always welcome in wider society. Seeing the negative effects of overindulgence led the Swiss government to heavily regulate alcohol throughout the 20th century.

THEOPRASTUS
BOMBAST von HOHENHEIM

otherwise known as

PARACELSUS

Switzerland's most famous alchemist was born at the end of the 15th century in Egg, a small village near the abbey of Einsiedeln. He spent much of his life wandering through different communities, speaking to everyday people, railing against the medical establishment, and practicing as a doctor and alchemist. With so much wandering, it's almost unbelievable that in his short 47 years he managed to write countless volumes on medicine, chemistry, the natural world, and even magic—in his time he was the second-most prolific scholar after Martin Luther.

Paracelsus encouraged doctors to better observe their patients and was a proponent of an evidence-based approach to medicine. He was skeptical of bloodletting and denounced the practice of applying cow paddies to heal wounds in favour of keeping them clean.

It was also Paracelsus who created laudanum, brought chemistry into medicine, and gave us the words chemistry, gas, and alcohol—which he borrowed from Arabic. "*Al*" simply meant "the" and "*kohl*" was the powdered essence left over after sublimating stibnite, which had been used as a cosmetic for centuries, notably in dark eye makeup. The kohl was essentially the spirit of the substance, just like the high proof alcohol was the spirit of the distilled wine.

GULDENWASSER

As an alchemist, Paracelsus was also interested in *Aurum Potable*, drinkable gold, thought to be the universal curative and possibly the elixir of life. The Little Bernese Cookbook of 1749 has a recipe for Guldenwasser, a dilution (both in name and substance) of "gold in water". According to the cookbook, a sober tablespoon of this spirit would awaken the brain, cure vertigo, open the lungs, ease labour pains...

I've updated it here, taking out some impossible to find and possibly poisonous ingredients (I'm looking at you creeping ivy), and can affirm that it does awaken the brain (and the back of the throat).

Of the herbs that are not marked in quantity, use about 5 grams each.

turmeric

grains of paradise

galangal

ginger

long pepper (pippali)

nutmeg

lavender

sage

5 juniper berries

3 bay leaves

2 cinnamon sticks

5 cloves

place herbs in a 1 litre bottle. Fill with kirsch and leave in a warm place for at least 2 weeks. Strain into a bottle.

REGULATING SPIRIT

These spirited additions to daily life were not universally accepted. In 1887, the Swiss Alcohol Board (SAB), a government department responsible for the production and distribution of hard alcohol and industrial ethanol (though not beer or wine), was formed.

The backlash against *Schnaps* had already begun decades before. In 1837, Heinrich Zschokke published the *Branntweinpest* (*The* Schnaps *Plague*) and two years later Jeremias Gotthelf wrote *Wie fünf Mädchen im Branntwein jämmerlich umkamen* (*How Five Girls Perished Miserably in* Schnaps). Alcohol abuse was seen as a problem of the working classes—farmers, factory workers, and the poor.

The SAB worked hard to promote the consumption of crops as food rather than alcoholic drinks. They incentivised making *Süssmost*—sweet, non-alcoholic apple juice—instead of distilling apples, and they ran ads promoting healthy eating in an attempt to encourage the Swiss public to eat their fruit and potatoes rather than distill them. "Eat an apple during your morning break!" declared one ad, with a row of smiling children biting into crisp fruit. Fruit and vegetables were the key to happiness and good health, and one campaign even proclaimed *Kartoffeln machen schlank* (potatoes make you slim) encouraging women to eat, rather than drink, their taters.

MOBILE DISTILLERIES

For most of the twentieth century Swiss farmers were only allowed to distill a certain amount of spirits based on the amount of cattle they had on the farm. The booze was meant to be used for farm purposes—when calves had colic, as a disinfectant or even, historically, to pay farm hands.

However, Swiss farmers didn't all have stills in their barns to turn their fruit into *Schnaps*. Instead, they depended on mobile distilleries—often big carts with stills on the back, pulled by horses or tractors.

After the fall harvest, the farmers would put their fruit in big barrels where it could rest and ferment. Between the New Year and the spring, travelling distilleries would go from farm to farm distilling this fermented mash into alcohol. For smaller operations it would take a day or so, but my father-in-law remembers the cart staying at his parent's farm for a whole week before all their fruit had been processed.

Some of these travelling distillers would be above-board, checking government cards as they went, and only distilling as much as each farm was allowed. But there were also black market distillers who would be willing to go over the allowed limit or secretly distill extra fruit.

Today these mobile distilleries still do exist in some form, though they distill much less than they used to. And they don't travel to each farm anymore, now they set up shop in one location and local farmers come to them, with their fermented mash in tow.

ABRICOTINE

Switzerland's favourite apricots come from the Valais, the warm wine producing region in the southwest of the country. They are the pride of Swiss fruit production, with stands selling the scarlet speckled fruit popping up throughout the country in July and August.

The most famous variety are the Luizet, named for the French horticulturist who developed them. They thrive in the warm, dry conditions of the Valais but their short season and delicate fruit mean that they are usually not transported very far from where they are picked.

It's this variety that is used to make Abricotine, the strong apricot spirit of the region. It's a protected product and for a producer to be able to use the name Abricotine, 90% of the fruits must be Luizet apricots, and all aspects of production must take place in the Valais.

MUNDER SAFRAN

High on a valasian mountain, is the tiny community of Mund, where they harvest no more than five kilos of saffron per year. Saffron grows from crocus flowers, each bloom yielding only three thin scarlet threads. It takes over a hundred flowers to make a single gram, which can cost upwards of 30 francs.

It's thought that during the Middle Ages the saffron was brought to Switzerland from Spain by pilgrims, who smuggled it into the country in their hair and beards.

Today it is as revered as ever, and you can purchase strands of saffron from Mund, as well as saffron Schnaps and liqueur.

A Bowle is the German version of punch. Depending on how sweet your wine is, you may need to add a little more or less elderflower syrup. The version on the following page.

ABRICOTINE SPRITZER

1 part Abricotine
2 threads of saffron
1 tbsp apricot jam
   (warmed and strained)
chilled, sparkling white wine

Steep the saffron in the
Abricotine for 10 minutes
Add the jam and top with wine.

APRICOT BOWLE

500g apricots,
sliced

200ml
Abricotine

1 litre
sparkling
water

100ml
elderflower
syrup

2 bottles
sparkling
wine

ABSINTHE

Absinthe originated in the Val-de-Travers, in the canton of Neuchâtel. It's made from a blend of anise, fennel, wormwood, and other botanicals.

absinthe's holy trinity

anise

fennel

wormwood

During the late 1800s absinthe became the drink of choice for the bohemians in Paris, and the likes of Baudelaire, Toulouse-Lautrec, Zola, and Gaugin imbibed the spirit, known as the green fairy.

Although many of its psychoactive properties were exaggerated (or can be attributed to the fact that many artists mixed their absinthe with laudanum and other drugs), the tide turned on absinthe at the start of the 20th century and tales of mania led to it being banned for almost a century.

In Switzerland, it was one farmer whose murderous rampage spurred the ban. Jean Lanfray came home drunk one afternoon and when his wife refused to polish his shoes, he shot her and their two young daughters with a shotgun. Two small glasses of absinthe were blamed, though Lanfray was a known inebriate who had already drunk over a litre of wine and numerous spirits before he arrived home.

Outrage about the case led to a popular vote in Switzerland on whether the government should ban the drink. In 1908, the vote passed with 63.5%, and many European and North American countries followed suit.

In the late 1990s and early 2000s absinthe had a revival in Europe and North America. In 2005, the Swiss repealed the earlier ban and absinthe was again made (legally) in its birthplace, the Val-de-Travers.

HOW TO SERVE ABSINTHE

You need:

a glass

sugar cubes

Absinthe
val de travers

cold water

an absinthe spoon
(or a fork)

sugar cubes

spoon

absinthe→

pour cold water through the sugar cubes

stir

This method is known as La Louche, French for opaque, because the clear liquid gets cloudy as the water is added

Although absinthe was banned for nearly a century, production never stopped in its birthplace, the Val de Travers. Stills remained in basements, and herbs—anise, fennel, wormwood— were dried in attics. If a formal complaint was lodged, the police would come to the house, destroy the sill, pour out the absinthe and punish the rogue distillers with fines or jail time.

ABSINTHE and MITTERAND

It was a big deal when Pierre Aubert, member of the Swiss federal counsel, invited French president François Mitterand to have lunch in Neuchâtel in 1983. It was France's first state visit to Switzerland since 1910 and the meal was meticulously planned, including the dessert *Soufleé glacé à la Fée Verte* (frozen soufleé à la green fairy). When the chef was interviewed about it on TV he gave up its "secret" ingredient—absinthe.

Still banned in Switzerland, the chef was eventually taken to court where he said that the dessert hadn't contained absinthe at all, but the anise flavoured Pastis. But now, instead of being charged for possession of absinthe, he was charged with fraud. Eventually he would be acquitted— two years later.

Here's a taste of Mitterand's dessert, without having to make a soufflé.

FRAPPÉ à la FÉE VERTE

200 mL milk
1 shot absinthe
1 shot Eierkirsch
1 scoop vanilla ice cream
Blend well.

Recipe for Eierkirsch on page 74

It was in New Orleans that absinthe was mixed into some of its finest cocktails. Here are two classics

SWISS SAZERAC

5 parts cognac
1 part absinthe
1 sugar cube
½ part alpenbitter
Stir over ice, then strain.

The milky green Suissesse is creamy and refreshing and makes an excellent brunch drink (or hair of the dog).

SUISSESSE

1 part crème de menthe
1 part absinthe
1 part cream
1 egg white
Shake over ice.

MONKEY GLAND

Monkey Gland is a 1920s cocktail whose name refers to the practice of grafting monkey testicles onto human testicles in an attempt at rejuvenation and improved virility (not to mention better memory, longer life, and improved vision).

This kind of surgery was the creation of Dr Serge Voronoff, a Russian-French surgeon who was interested in glands and hormones and how they influenced the ageing process. He had come to France as a young man to study medicine, and later found himself in North Africa observing the effect of castration on eunuchs. Early in his career he experimented by injecting himself with ground up guinea pig and dog testicles, but when this did not produce his expected results, he started grafting actual squares of monkey gland onto humans.

People loved it.

His process was extremely popular and made him a very wealthy man. He even had his very own monkey farm to support his surgeries.

Although the placebo effect allowed a form of rejuvenation in some of his patients (or so they believed), it became obvious that his technique could not give his patients the results they desired. He quickly fell out of favour, as did his techniques.

The Monkey Gland, his namesake cocktail, has two Swiss connections—the green fairy herself, absinthe, and the fact that Serge Voronoff died in Lausanne in 1951.

MONKEY GLAND

5 parts gin

3 parts orange juice

splash absinthe

splash grenadine

shake with ice

strain into a martini glass

Absinthe for what ails you

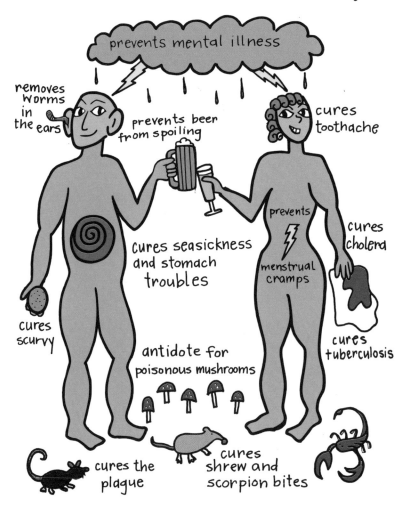

prevents mental illness

removes worms in the ears

prevents beer from spoiling

cures toothache

cures seasickness and stomach troubles

prevents menstrual cramps

cures cholera

cures scurvy

antidote for poisonous mushrooms

cures tuberculosis

cures the plague

cures shrew and scorpion bites

Over the centuries, people have praised and denounced absinthe for the effect it has on the human body. It has been seen as both a cure and cause for mental illness and numerous other disorders. But before it was condemned as an instrument for murder, absinthe, and more generally wormwood, were said to have curative properties.

Absinthe was perhaps never enjoyed as much as during the *Belle-Epoque*, at another icon of the time, The Ritz Hotel, Paris.

CÉSAR RITZ

César Ritz was born in 1850 in Niederwald in Valais, the last of thirteen children and extremely poor. With ingenuity and exacting standards, he went from those humble beginnings to having his very name be a synonym for unabashed luxury.

As he ascended from waiter to hotel manager, anecdotes about his ingenuity abounded. While managing a hotel on the Rigi-Kulm, the heating went out just before a lunch for 40 wealthy American guests. To warm the room he had copper palm pots emptied, filled with oil, and set alight. Then he placed warm, blanket-wrapped bricks at the feet of each guest.

He championed hygienic practices in hotels and his were the very first to have private ensuite bathrooms in each room. To flatter the complexions, and accent the jewellery of his clients, he used indirect lighting, as well as pale peach and gold tones that still exist in many Ritz dining rooms today. Less flattering was Edward VII, Prince of Wales, who got stuck in the bathtub he was sharing with a lady friend, leading Ritz to invent a king-sized tub for his portly guest. It was Ritz who supposedly gave Grand Marnier its name, so it's fitting that it features in his own luxury cocktail.

the RITZ

3 parts cognac
2 parts Grand Marnier
2 parts orange juice
Stir over ice.
Top with champagne.

the KRONENHALLE

One of Zürich's most famous restaurant bars, the Kronenhalle, has hosted the likes of James Joyce, Pablo Picasso, Andy Warhol, Catherine Deneuve, Placido Domingo, Coco Chanel and Lauren Bacall—even Swiss literary kings Friedrich Dürrenmatt and Max Frisch were regulars.

In 1984, Kronenhalle head bartender Peter Roth developed the Ladykiller, a strong fruity drink that won the World Cocktail Championship and made its way into the canon.

LADYKILLER

2 parts gin
1 part orange liqueur
1 part apricot brandy
4 parts passionfruit juice
4 parts pineapple juice
Shake over ice.
Garnish with orange peel, cherries and mint.

HARRY SCHRAEMLI

There was one man who worked tirelessly to bring American cocktail culture to Switzerland, Harry Schraemli.

With a long career in the hospitality industry (at 26 he was the youngest hotel manager of his time), he also wrote passionately about food and drink. Most notable is his *Das Grosse Lehrbuch der Bar* ("The Big Bar Manual") first published in the 1940s, which became the standard book for Swiss hospitality students learning mixology and bartending.

In the book, Schraemli lays out everything you need for the smooth handling of a bar—a inventory of correct glasses, suggestions for modest food offerings, what to look for in barmen and barmaids, how to stock a wine cellar, a selection of toasts in English, descriptions of pretty much every bottled drink that existed at the time, and recipes for all standard cocktails, plus a few of his own creations.

My favourite Harry Schraemli drink is undoubtedly his gorgeous Violetta cocktail. Recipe for Eierkirsch on page 74.

VIOLETTA

1 part cassis

1 part cream

1 part Eierkirsch

Shake well over ice.

ALPENBITTER

peppermint

gentian root

juniper

anise

Alpenbitter is a strong, bitter spirit flavoured with herbs. The most famous variety in Switzerland is Appenzeller.

Its founder was Emil Ebneter, who experimented with different local herbs, interested in their medicinal properties. Eventually he opened a shop, patented the name, joined forces with his brother-in-law Beat Kölbener, relocated to a bigger distillery (the same as today), asked his local monks to lend their herbal know-how, and ended up winning the gold medal for his bitter at the Swiss Expo in 1914.

The company remains a family affair, and today it's just one member of each family (Ebneter and Kölbener) who know the secret recipe.

Sorry, American friends, but you won't find Appenzeller in your liquor stores—it can't be imported into the United States because some of the forty-two herbs are not approved by America's Food and Drug Administration.

But what doesn't kill you might potentially settle your stomach. Appenzeller purportedly has curative properties and, like other herbal digestifs, it's a good choice after a big meal.

APPENZELLER eiskaffe

whipped
cream

1 shot
Appenzeller

cup of
offee

a big scoop of
vanilla or
coffee
ice cream

Stir well.

BITTER des DIABLERETS

Although Appenzeller is undoubtedly the most famous of all the Swiss *Alpenbitters*, other versions are made throughout the country, with each producer using their own distinct mix of herbs.

One such example is Bitter des Diablerets, whose legend goes like this:

In the 18th century, the devil thought he would amuse himself by throwing rocks, causing landslides in the tiny village of Derborence, high in the Valais. The village was destroyed, but the buried peasants survived by sucking the alpine herbs for sustence. The mountains were renamed *Diablerets* (home of the devil) after their cloven-footed foe, and the bitters, made with those same alpine herbs, took on this name as well.

Bitter des Diablerets can be drunk alone or mixed with cola or other fizzy drinks. Mixed with classic Swiss soda, Elmer Citro (use Sprite or 7up if you can't find Elmer), it's citrusy with a bitter bite.

DIABLE AMER

2 parts Bitter des Diablerets

1 part lime juice

5 parts Elmer Citro

Stir over ice.

My friends at zur Alten Weinhandlung in Trubschachen like their *Alpenbitter* (preferably from canton Glarus) with a dash of the green fairy.

MITTE DRINK

3 parts alpenbitter
1 part absinthe
Stir over ice.

To garnish, lightly toast a branch of rosemary then swirl it into the drink.

Amateur mixologist and brain scientist Dr. Richard McKinley introduced me to this version, which replaces Campari with *Alpenbitter*.

ALPENBITTER NEGRONI

1 part gin
1 part sweet vermouth
1 part alpenbitter
Stir over ice.

ALPINE SCHNAPS

The woodsy, pine smell from many alpine dwellings likely comes from furniture made from *Pinus Cembra or Arven,* Swiss pine. This tree, which grows throughout the Alps and Carpathian mountains, has been known to have therapeutic properties for centuries. Even sleeping in a bed made from its wood is said to lower your heart rate. Of course, its curative properties can also be imbibed, and many alpine dwellers, especially those in Grisons, make a spirit from its pinecones.

make your own ARVENSCHNAPS

 In late June/early July, harvest 3-4 pinecones from a Swiss pine.

Slice into rounds

 Place in a large glass jar with 500mL kirsch. Cover and leave in a warm place for a few months. Strain and fill into a bottle.

Other spirits from the alpine realm include *Enzian*, a *Schnaps* made from the gentian root (a plant also present in Angostura bitters), and *Genepi*, which is a sweetened liqueur made from wormwood. Some even make *Schnaps* from the beloved, furry edelweiss.

IVA SCHNAPS

Iva Schnaps has been made for centuries in Grisons from the Iva plant (Iva in Romansch, with the romantic English name of "simple-leaved milfoil") that grows happily 2000m above sea level. Initially made in private homes, it was the *Zuckerbäcker*, those intrepid young men who left their rustic upbringings to traverse the continent working in bakeries and pastry shops, who commercialised the drink and sold it on their travels. It was embraced by many, especially the Italians, who liked its acetic taste. Extremely bitter, and mostly drunk alone, it pairs well with sweet vermouth or orange juice.

IVA ORANGE

1 part iva schnaps
1 part orange liqueur
4 parts orange juice
Stir over ice.
Top with sparkling water.

BRÄCHETE

Before the ease of readily available cotton, Swiss farm families would make linen by hand by processing flax. The breaking, or *Brächete* as it was called, was a day-long event that villages in the Emmental would host.

Using large wooden implements, the flax would be combed, roasted, rolled through a large wooden crushing machine, pounded by hand, combed again, rinsed, and spun into threads as fine as hair. Finally it could be woven into all manner of products, from tablecloths to *Trachten* (traditional Swiss dresses). No part of the flax went to waste and by-products were used for house and pipe insulation, as well as in sausage making.

All this hard work demanded a proper reward at the end of the day and that came via a strong caramel *Schnaps*—Brächere Brönnts—named for the event where it was served. As dusk fell, the exhausted flax breakers would imbibe the rejuvenating liquid, play their accordions, and dance into the night. Love also blossomed, as the villagers waited to see what young man carried home which young lady's spinning wheel.

Serve your Brächere Brönnts straight or mix it into cinnamon tea.

BRÄCHERE BRÖNNTS

caramelize the sugar

When it turns golden, remove from heat nd add 200ml water.

WATCH OUT!

It will splutter.

Put the pot back over medium heat and cook until all the sugar dissolves in the water

Add:

3 cloves

3 juniper berries

1 tsp caraway seeds

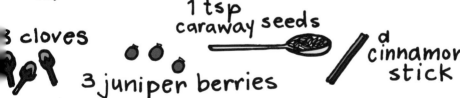

a cinnamon stick

et sit 10 minutes.
Stir in 400ml Kirsch then strain into bottles. Makes 500ml.

CHRÜTER

Kräuterschnaps (herb *Schnaps*), is a twice-distilled spirit flavoured with a mix of herbs and spices. The process is simple: distill a spirit—apple, pear, or quince will do—then mix in caraway and anise and a secret formulation of herbs and spices. Distill again and voila, *Chrüter.*

Chrüter isn't just for the liquor cabinet—it can also be found in the medicine cabinet and applied liberally to bad moods, sore stomachs, and other digestive problems.

ALTE CHRÜTER

There is also Alte (old) *Chrüter.* Roasted wood chips and a bit of sugar are added to regular *Chrüter,* creating a sweeter, more flavourful, and slightly milder drink.

BÜRGERMEISTERLI

The Basel version of *Chrüter* is named after the former *Bürgermeister* (mayor) of the city, who made his own herby spirit at the end of the 18th century.

CHÜMMI/ÄNTÄBÜSI

Flavoured with *Kümmel* (caraway), this *Schnaps* is popular throughout central Switzerland. My in-laws drink a version called *Äntäbüsi,* a dialect name which literally means duck, *Ente*, and cat, *Büsi*, (I came across one complicated origin story about feuding farmers, a caraway windfall, and a cat that lived in harmony with ducks).

HEUSCHNAPS

Some *Schnaps* also add hay (*Heu*) as a flavouring. *Heuschnaps* from the Wetterhorn Hotel in Hasliberg is made according to a decades old recipe that was found in the hotel basement, and uses fresh alpine hay.

Verdauerli is simply the Swiss German word for digestif—a small tipple to take after a
[bi]g meal to help with the *Verdauung* (digestion). A variation on the theme is this warm
[dr]ink that contains the digestive magic of tea, honey, and herby booze.

[T]EE VERDAUERLI

1 cup peppermint
or fennel tea

1 tsp honey

1 shot chrüter

[K]CHÜMMI

1 tbsp
caraway
seeds,
crushed

2 tbsp
sugar

500mL

Kirsch

[S]hake well, then
[l]eave in a warm
[p]lace for 2 weeks.
[S]train into a bottle.

GRAPPA

In winemaking, once the grapes have been pressed, the parts that remain are often themselves distilled. The leftover skins and seeds, called pomace in English, are distilled into *Marc*. Or you might be more familiar with the Italian name, grappa.

Now protected throughout Europe, grappa can only be produced in Italy, Ticino, or San Marino. Grappa has been produced in Ticino since at least the 1800s, where it was made in Santa Maria del Bigorio, a Capuchin monastery founded in 1535. Though initially of low-quality and favoured by the working classes, today grappa is carefully distilled from high-quality grapes and considered a luxury product, beloved in the region and the rest of the country. Often in Ticino it's made with a strain of the region's *uva americana* (American grapes) that lend a notable musky taste to the spirit.

GRAPPA ALEXANDER

1 part Grappa
1 part crème de cacao
1 part cream

Shake with ice.
Garnish with nutmeg

HÄRDÖPFLER

Also known as *Kartoffelbrand*, potato *Schnaps* has been distilled in Switzerland since the 1800s. Easy to grow and cheaper than wine, potatoes were the most popular choice for distilling, at a time when hard liquor was consumed at a much higher rate than today.

For many who lived in poverty, *Härdöpfler* provided not only a way to still hunger pangs, but also to escape a bleak existence.

But the government was concerned.

Potatoes were a nutritious, complex carbohydrate, and the government saw their metamorphosis into booze as a threat to the food supply. Shortly after the First World War, the government banned the use of potatoes as a *Schnaps* base. But, much like absinthe, many people continued to distill their tubers in secret. It wasn't until almost the 21st century that it could legally be produced again.

The bottles you can buy today proudly display their starchy origin and some even boast a light potato-y taste. Mainly for drinking neat, it is said to help digestion and protect against the flu.

Some people swear by their daily shot of potato.

KIRSCH

Made from cherries, kirsch is Switzerland's most famous spirit. It has a long history, both as a favoured tipple gracing soldiers' flasks and hiking rucksacks, and an enemy of the temperance movement who saw the damage kirsch could do to heavy imbibers.

It was the crusaders who brought cherry trees to Switzerland from the Middle East, and these still blossom throughout the country. Kirsch is made in most regions, most famously in cantons Basel and Zug.

In central Switzerland alone, there are over three hundred varieties of cherry—and over eight hundred in the whole country. For one litre of kirsch, upwards of 3000 cherries are needed, depending on the sort. The cherries are fermented with their stones, which can give the kirsch a light almond taste.

Owing to its relatively neutral flavour, kirsch is often used in cooking and baking, featuring in numerous cakes, such as the famous *Zuger Kirschtorte* and Black Forest Cake, as well as confections like *Kirschstängeli*, booze filled chocolate sticks. Most famously, it's added to cheese fondue and some people even have little shot glasses of kirsch next to their plates to dunk the bread in before dipping it into the cheese.

ZUGER KIRSCHTORTE

½ part kirsch
1 part cherry liqueur
1 part amaretto
1 part cream
shake over ice.

BLACK FOREST CAKE

½ part kirsch
1 part cherry liqueur
1 part crème de cacao
1 part cream
shake over ice.

ROSE

½ part strawberry syrup
1 part kirsch
2 parts dry vermouth
shake over ice.

If you don't have strawberry syrup to make this classic cocktail, use
another red syrup—grenadine, cherry, raspberry—or a reddish fruit
liqueur like Röteli or Chambord.

EIERKIRSCH

Eierkirsch is a kirsch-based drink with added eggs, cream, and sugar. Today it's especially loved at Christmas, when it can be spiced with cinnamon and nutmeg.

Produced on the same farms that would grow the cherries needed for kirsch, the addition of eggs and sugar was possibly not only to create a pleasing taste, but also to provide protein and energy for the labourers who worked the fields.

My mother-in-law Josy fondly remembers drinking cold, refreshing *Eierkirsch* during the *Heuen*, when her family would cut and dry the hay for the cows.

One mixed drink that uses *Eierkirsch* is the boozy, noggy Snowball.

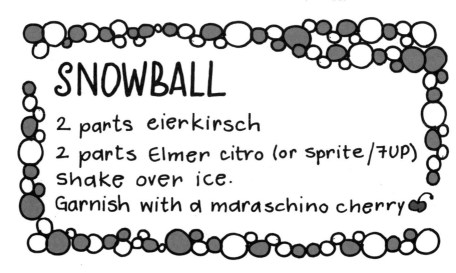

SNOWBALL
2 parts eierkirsch
2 parts Elmer citro (or Sprite/7UP)
Shake over ice.
Garnish with a maraschino cherry

HOW TO MAKE EIERKIRSCH

In a bowl, over a pot of simmering water, whisk together:

4 egg yolks

50 ml milk

30 g condensed milk (In Switzerland this is sold in tubes)

1 vanilla bean (scraped) or 1 tbsp vanilla paste or extract

bowl should not touch the water

simmering water

Keep whisking until the liquid is slightly thickened and hot to the touch.

Whisk in 200ml Kirsch.

Strain into bottles and store in the fridge for up to a month.
Makes about 500ml.
Shake well before serving.

KIRSCH

homemade eier-kirsch

NOCINO

Nocino is a bittersweet liqueur made from green walnuts and particularly enjoyed in Ticino. Though it's not unique to that region, it's possible that it has been produced there in monasteries since the 1500s. Walnut spirits are popular throughout Europe, and the ticinese variety was probably introduced from Italy.

Like their famous chestnuts, walnuts also grow plentifully in Italian Switzerland, and at one time they were an essential product. Walnut oil was used not only for cooking, but also as lamp oil. The advent of electricity and availability of other cooking oils may have reduced the importance of the trees, but also freed up more nuts to be used for booze.

Nocino is made by soaking green walnuts in spirit (usually grappa) until the liquid turns black and bitter, then adding sugar and spices to make a complex, nutty, bittersweet drink. Its production is linked to the Feast of St John on the 24 June. On the eve of that day, the monks would harvest the unripe nuts and set to work steeping.

Sometimes Nocino is referred to as *ratafià*, which is actually a larger category of drink, and seems to encompass many different spirits created by soaking fruits, nuts, and spices. The word *ratafià* comes from the Latin rata fiat (done deal, ratified) and signified the spirit that was imbibed after a contract or agreement had been signed.

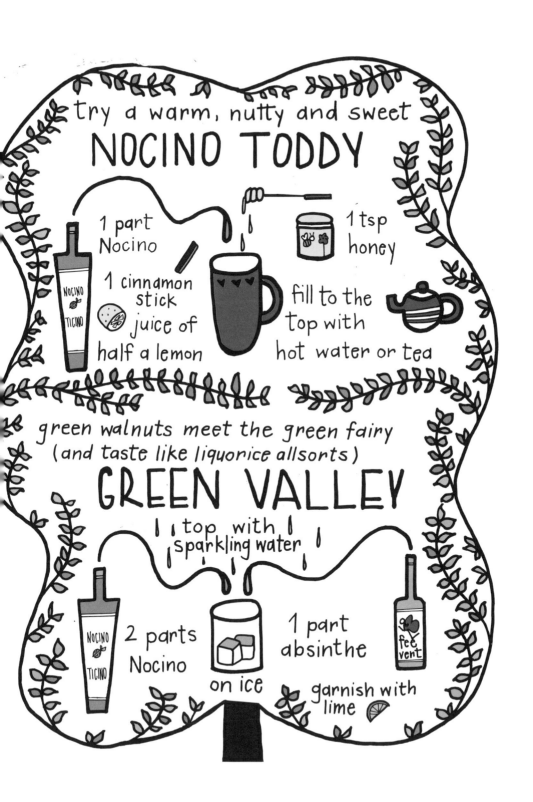

try a warm, nutty and sweet

NOCINO TODDY

1 part
Nocino

1 cinnamon
stick
juice of
half a lemon

1 tsp
honey

fill to the
top with
hot water or tea

green walnuts meet the green fairy
(and taste like liquorice allsorts)

GREEN VALLEY

top with
sparkling water

2 parts
Nocino

on ice

1 part
absinthe

garnish with
lime

RÖTELI

Röteli is a liqueur made with dried cherries and spices that dates from at least the 19th century. It was traditionally made by families in Grisons, each using a different spice mixture. In the early 1900s, traditional recipes were collected and experimented with, leading to a standardized version that could be mass-produced.

It's traditional to drink *Röteli* on New Year's Eve. In the olden days, bachelors would take this occasion to go from farmhouse to farmhouse visiting unmarried farmer's daughters. At each farm they would sample a glass of *Röteli* that the single ladies (under the watchful eye of their mothers) had made.

Some saw the drink as a kind of love potion, and often these visits would result in marriage proposals. The further back in the valley the bachelors went, the drunker they got, and the better looking and more appealing the daughters became, giving a big advantage to those who lived in remote farmhouses.

CHERRY COLA FLOAT

1 shot Röteli

1 scoop vanilla ice cream

Top with cola.

BÜNDNER RIVELLA

2 shots Röteli
Rivella

Stir over ice.
Garnish with lemon.

MAKING SPIRITS

My sister-in-law Franziska works for Distillery Studer in Escholzmatt, a family run company since 1883 and home to numerous award-winning spirits.

Escholzmatt in the late 1800s and early 1900s was a typical small Swiss town. The people went to church on Sunday and while the wives hurried back home to prepare Sunday lunch, their husbands perched in the local *Beiz* (restaurant), having a short aperitif of Träsch or kirsch—a whole 100ml per person.

Today the market for these traditional Swiss spirits is shrinking as new generations are choosing gin and rum over Williams and Zwetschgen. However, small distilleries like Studer are keeping the tradition alive with continued production of high quality fruit spirits alongside a broader selection of other booze.

The delightful distillery manager and owner, Ivano Friedli-Studer, likes a cool Williams Tonic on a hot summer's day.

STUDER WILLIAMS TONIC
1 part Williams
top with tonic water
Rub the rim with a lemon slice
and squeeze into the glass.
Serve over ice.

TRÄSCH

Träsch in Swiss German, or *Bätzi* in Bernese German, is a spirit distilled from apples and pears. Both names refer to fruit leftovers—*Bätzi* which can mean apple core, and *Träsch* from *Trester*, the leftover parts of the fruits once they've been pressed for juice or oil. Similarly, apple and pear spirits would be distilled from the leftover *Most* (cider). Today, typically the whole fruit is used.

WILLIAM TELL

1 part cinnamon syrup
1 part lemon juice
2 parts Träsch
Shake over ice.
Top with saurer most (dry apple cider)

APPLE SHOT

half träsch
half süssmost
(sweet apple cider)
sprinkle with cinnamon

Recipe for Cinnamon Syrup on page 85.

WILLIAMS

Basically any food or drink in Switzerland with Williams in the name means that it contains pear or pear *Schnaps*.

This is down to the name of the pear itself, the Williams pear (Bartlett in North America) which, with a firm-ish texture and juicy inside, lends itself well to cooking and processing. The pears carry the surname of Williams, the English gardener who popularized them in the UK. Later, an American named Enoch Bartlett acquired a piece of property in Massachusetts full of Williams pear trees that had been brought over from England. He didn't know their provenance, so he simply named the variety after himself. It wasn't until decades later in the early 1800s that people realized that the two pears were the same variety.

PEARS in BOTTLES

Williams pears are the basis for the *Schnaps* of the same name, and it was the Germarnier family in canton Valais who first had the idea of enhancing their pear spirit by growing an entire pear inside the liquor bottle. The Germarniers carefully placed their bottle over tiny pear blossoms and let the pear grow inside, gently removing it once the fruit was ripe. Although today there are knockoffs with false bottoms allowing fully grown pears to be added, some distilleries in Switzerland, France, and Germany still practice the original method.

Once you've finished your bottle, don't be tempted to break it open and fish out the pear—by that time it doesn't have any flavour and smashing the bottle makes quite a mess.

GINGER WILLIAMS

part williams
tsp vanilla paste or extract
Stir over ice.
Top with ginger ale.

PEAR SOUR

parts williams
parts lemon juice
part elderflower syrup
egg white
Shake over ice.

MARETTO PERA

parts williams
part lemon juice
part amaretto
Shake over ice.

ZWETSCHGEN

Pflümli and *Zwetschgen* both refer to spirits m
from plums, *Pflümli* typically designating ro
plums, and *Zwetschge* the oval variety. After cherr
plums are the most popular stone fruit for distil
in Switzerland. Many varieties exist—including sp
made from little golden mirabelles, the *Chézard*
Bérudge plums from Neuchâtel, and *Zyberli* from
Entlebuch. There is also the *Vieille Prune*, a vers
that is sweetened and aged in barrels, producir
fragrant, golden spirit.

DAMASSINE

One of Switzerland's finest plum brandies co
from the Jura, where they grow little red pl
called Red Damasson. As the name hints, they w
brought back by the crusaders—Damasson, like
city of Damascus.

Grown throughout the region, particularly in the A
these little ruby plums produce a superb *eau-de*
In the early 2000s, Damassine was granted prote
status with strict guidelines about how the spirit
be made, including a stipulation that the trees mus
picked by hand and not shaken.

Zwetschgen can be replaced with any kind of p
Schnaps in the following recipes.

PLUM SOUR

3 parts zwetschgen
2 parts lemon juice
1 part cinnamon syrup
1 egg white
Shake over ice.
Sprinkle with cinnamon.

PLUM STINGER

1 part zwetschgen
1 part crème de menthe
Stir over ice.

CINNAMON SYRUP

200 ml water
200 g sugar
Bring to a boil and
dissolve all sugar.
Take off heat and
add 4 cinnamon sticks.
Cover the pot and let sit until cool. 
Strain and keep in the fridge for
up to 3 weeks. Makes about 300ml.

STAYING WARM
on the slopes

The combinations of booze, sugar, warm liquids and cream served on Swiss ski hills are endless.

Whether you drink them for après-ski, or you skip the skiing altogether, these warm, spirited concoctions are bound to warm your belly.

GLETSCHERWASSER

lemon

lemon juice

hot water

zwetschgen

BOMBARDINO

cinnamon

whipped cream

Eierkirsch

Brandy

SCHOGGI mit SCHUSS

whipped cream

hot chocolate

booze of your choosing*

* Bailey's, rum, amaretto crème de menthe, cointreau

how to ORDER BOOZY COFFEE

coffee

booze of your choosing

In German Switzerland,

Kafischnaps

or

Kafi Fertig

are generic terms for boozy coffee.

Kafi Chrüter adds herbal spirits

Kafi GT adds cream

Order a **Cheli** and your drink may come in a chaceli →

a traditional way to serve the drink (especially in Obwalden).

In Ticino, ordering

Caffé coretto

or

caffé grappa

puts a tipple in your brew.

Kafi Träsch* means your drink is spiked with this central Swiss favourite. You'll probably find it in your **Kafi Luz/Lutz** too.

* Träsch, an apple and pear spirit

In French Switzerland, just ask for your coffee with your desired spirit:

café kirsch   **café prune**

The stakes are higher with a *Flämmli*, especially if you've already had a few. It's basically a boozy coffee, set aflame. A poorly-orchestrated one probably won't result in scorched eyebrows, but it might split your cup clean in half.

Williams is the traditional spirit, but other high proof varieties work too. Some might argue that the traditional serving vessel is the classic Swiss coffee glass.

HOW TO SERVE FLÄMMLI
without cracking your cup

Add 2 tsp sugar

or 2 sugar cubes

to an espresso

DO NOT STIR!

Drink out the espresso, leaving the sugar undissolved at the bottom of the cup.

dd a hot of lliams

take a bit of booze out with your spoon

light it on fire

tip the booze back in— FIRE!

lift sugar into the flame to let it caramelize

put out the flame with the saucer or your flat palm

let cool, then enjoy.

ÄNTLIBUECHER KAFI

Let's talk about the real reason many Swiss attend cold outdoor events: *Kafischnaps* (exactly what it sounds like, coffee laced with *Schnaps*).

A light coffee base, a good splash of spirits, a cube of sugar, and maybe a drop of cream or milk. One method has you toss a *Füfliber* (5-franc coin) into the bottom of the glass, fill it up with coffee until you can't see it anymore, then add the *Schnaps* until you can see it again.

The people of the Entlebuch are great consumers and probable originators of the drink, theirs known as *Äntlibuecher Kafi* or *Schwarze*.

My friend Friedrich Studer, born and raised in the heart of the region, declares it as much a part of his homeland as the landscape. He gives the history as follows: as soon as coffee drinking had been established in the city, the rural folk took up the habit and adapted it to their liking. This meant brewing weaker coffee (saving on expensive beans) and adding booze (personal preference). Although the moral authorities of the time criticised what they considered their lavishness, this didn't stop the Entlebuchers.

Kafischnaps goes hand in hand with farming in the region—brewed not only for farmers, but also for their cattle—but you don't need to live on a farm to drink it. *Kafischnaps* is ever-present at every *Fasnacht*, festival, *Alpabzug*, and hunting trip.

Here's a tip from Friedrich. He says that the best way to drink *Kafischnaps* is in a hut in a forest, with a wood-fired stove, and a bunch of good friends.

Not only did Friedrich give me the lowdown on *Äntlibuecher Kafi*, he also gave me his recipe. The *Schwarze* should contain so much booze that it's

SCHWARZE

Heat
1 handful coffee

ground   or   instant)

1 litre water

fir branch

stir

Drop the branch in and boil for a minute, then take it out, take the coffee off the heat and let it sit for a moment. Once the grounds have settled to the bottom, ladle the coffee off the top (or you can filter it, if you prefer). With instant, just make sure it's dissolved.

Now ddd sugar   and booze

kirsch

träsch

Zwiätschgje

williams

Buurehof news

cow milk

man!

no!   made

exclusive

the tables have turned...

RECIPE TIPS

Many of the recipes in this book are measured in parts, allowing you to easily adjust the quantity. A good tool is a jigger, or a shot glass with measurements on the side.

jigger

For the recipes that mention shaking, you will need a cocktail shaker and ice.

cocktail shaker

When making infused spirits or syrups, use clean bottles. You can rinse them out first with hot water or run them through the dishwasher. Syrups keep in the fridge for a few weeks and spirits will keep in the liquor cabinet almost indefinitely.

When straining syrups, use a metal sieve, but with the infused spirits, your best bet is cheesecloth or another very fine mesh.

My default *Schnaps* base is a standard kirsch, which has little flavour. You can also use other high-alcohol, low-flavour spirits like vodka or *Träsch*.

RESOURCES

There are many great resources if you are interested in learning more about Swiss drinking culture. The Swiss government website has all the statistics related to beverage consumption, as well as an archive of laws relating to alcohol.

In 2016, the government published a detailed book *Rausch & Ordnung / Ivresse & Ordre / Ebbrezza e Ordine* about the entire history of the Swiss Alcohol Board (1887-2015). It's filled with photos, statistics, and meticulous history, and can be ordered on the government's website.

Of course, there is also the online Culinary Heritage of Switzerland (*Kulinarisches Erbe der Schweiz / Patrimoine Culinaire Suisse / Patrimonio Culinario Svizzero*), the astounding collection of information about traditional and historic Swiss food and drink products.

♥MERCI VIEL MAL♥

Firstly, thanks to the team at Bergli. Richard and Satu, thank you for all your support and hard work. And to Kim, thank you for putting it all together so beautifully.

Friedrich, thank you for your reflections on Äntlibuecher Kafi. It's always a joy to drink with you (and Carmen (and Raphi) too).

Richard—thanks for preparing me my first ever breakfast martini with jam. Here's to being one of the best, and classiest, drinking buddies ever. Same goes for you Mary—and here's to much more merrymaking (and thank you for your sharp editor's eye).

Uncle Stuart, thank you so much for your invaluable editing, and for your presence at many drink tastings.

I couldn't do it without you Allie! Thank you for your skilled, critical eye and your unfailing support.

Johanna, thanks for asking around in the Romandie, and Heddi, my fellow Swiss food lover, thanks for reminding me about municipal wine.

Herzlichen Dank, Herr Friedli-Studer, dass ich Ihre wunderbare Destillerie besuchen und mit Ihnen reden konnte.

Danke, Barbara für die Lektion über Holdrio, und Vreni, ganz herzlichen Dank für die Auskunft über das Tessin.

Merci Fränzi für alles (nicht nur alle Schnapsfläschli). Ich denke immer an Dich, wenn ich muess, ich muess, ich muess es Schnäpseli ha.

Danke Robi und Josy, ich habe so viel über Kafischnaps und Milchkaffee (und mehr!) gelernt. Es freute mich sehr, dass ihr mir über eure Kindheit erzählt habt.

Mum, thanks for letting me ply you with drinks. Thank you for always taking such good care of us.

Thanks Sam, here's that creative director credit. Thanks for showing me the wide world of whisky, sour beer, and yogi drinks (in that order), and for winning me over to the good coffee maker.

And finally, a hearty *Zum Wohl* for Stella, the baby who could cheers before she could walk.

INDEX

INDEX

RULES for RAISING GLASSES

I was threatened with seven years of bad sex the first time I drank before the toast at a Swiss party. In Canada it's no sin to drink before saying cheers, but in Switzerland there are a few rules that go along with the clinking of glasses.

Once you receive your drink, you must not take a single sip until the toast is over and everyone has clinked glasses.

Make eye contact and say the person's name as you clink.

It may seem overly formal, but this acknowledgement of your fellow drinkers is a way to show respect to the host and other guests.

So whether you say *Proscht, Zum Wohl, Santé, Salute, or Viva,* Swiss drinks are definitely worth the ritual.

CHEERS!